HOW-TO LIBRARY

CRAFTING WITH WASHI TAPE

Written and Illustrated by Kathleen Petelinsek

CHERRY LAKE PUBLISHING • ANN ARBOR, MICHIGAN

CHERRY LAKE
Publishing

Published in the United States of America by Cherry Lake Publishing
Ann Arbor, Michigan
www.cherrylakepublishing.com

Photo Credits: Page 4, ©Christian Bertrand/Shutterstock.com; page 5, ©Bohbeh/Shutterstock.com; page 6, ©joppo/Shutterstock.com; page 7, ©Rafa Perdomo/Dreamstime.com.

Library of Congress Cataloging-in-Publication Data
Petelinsek, Kathleen.
  Crafting with washi tape / by Kathleen Petelinsek.
     pages cm
  Includes bibliographical references and index.
  ISBN 978-1-63137-778-5 (lib. bdg.) — ISBN 978-1-63137-838-6 (e-book)
— ISBN 978-1-63137-798-3 (pbk.) — ISBN 978-1-63137-818-8 (pdf)
 1. Tape craft. 2. Gummed paper tape. 3. Masking tape. 4. Japanese paper. I. Title.

TT869.7.P58 2015
736'.98—dc23   2014003983

Cherry Lake Publishing would like to acknowledge the work of The Partnership for 21st Century Skills. Please visit www.p21.org for more information.

Printed in the United States of America
Corporate Graphics Inc.
July 2014

TABLE OF CONTENTS

What Is Washi Tape?

Washi tape comes in a huge variety of colors and patterns.

Washi is a traditional, handmade type of Japanese paper. Today, it is often used to make **adhesive** tape for craft projects. The tape comes in a wide variety of colors and patterns. It can be as strong as duct tape, but the adhesive does not leave a sticky residue behind. This means you can tear it, write on it, move it, and reuse it. Washi tape is perfect for crafting projects because it can be pulled up without ruining the item it was placed on.

Washi is produced using fewer chemicals than other types of paper. This process results in crisper, smoother paper, but it takes longer than normal paper production. Washi paper **pulp** can be made from a variety of sources. It is often made from the bark of native Japanese trees and shrubs. It can also be made from other **renewable** fibers, such as bamboo, hemp, rice, or wheat. Both the process and the fibers used to make washi are environmentally friendly.

If you go to a craft store, you will probably find an entire section devoted to washi tape. Washi tape is perfect for wrapping presents or scrapbooking. As you will see in this book, it is also good for many other craft projects.

Bamboo is a tall, sturdy type of grass that is used to make washi tape and many other products.

How Did the Washi Phenomenon Start?

Painter's tape helps painters avoid getting paint in spots where they don't want it.

Kamoi Kakoshi is a Japanese company that has been making washi tape for more than 90 years. Originally, the tape was used much like painter's tape or masking tape, when people painted houses, cars, and furniture. It did not come in the wide variety of colors and patterns it does today.

In 2006, three women from Tokyo had an idea. They put together a book illustrating the wide variety of artistic uses for washi tape. They then e-mailed Kamoi Kakoshi and asked for a factory tour. They brought their book to show to the company's leaders and asked if the company would make its tape in more colors. Kamoi Kakoshi's leaders liked the idea. They had never realized their tape could be used in such beautiful ways.

In 2008, Kamoi Kakoshi launched washi tape in 20 different "artist colors." The new colors were a huge hit. Washi tape is now sold around the world in a **palette** of colors and patterns that is almost endless.

Today, many people keep washi tape among their household craft supplies.

Basic Materials

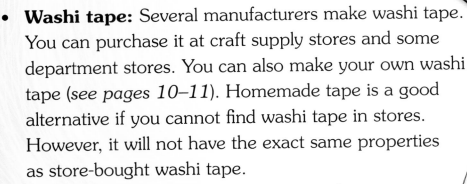

You will need to collect some basic materials before getting started with washi tape crafts. Below is a list of items that are necessary for most of the projects in this book. Check the instructions for each project to see if any other materials are needed.

- **Washi tape:** Several manufacturers make washi tape. You can purchase it at craft supply stores and some department stores. You can also make your own washi tape (*see pages 10–11*). Homemade tape is a good alternative if you cannot find washi tape in stores. However, it will not have the exact same properties as store-bought washi tape.
- **Scissors:** You will need scissors in order to cut and trim washi tape for different projects.
- **Things to decorate:** There is no need to buy new items for your washi tape projects. Simply use whatever you can find around your home.

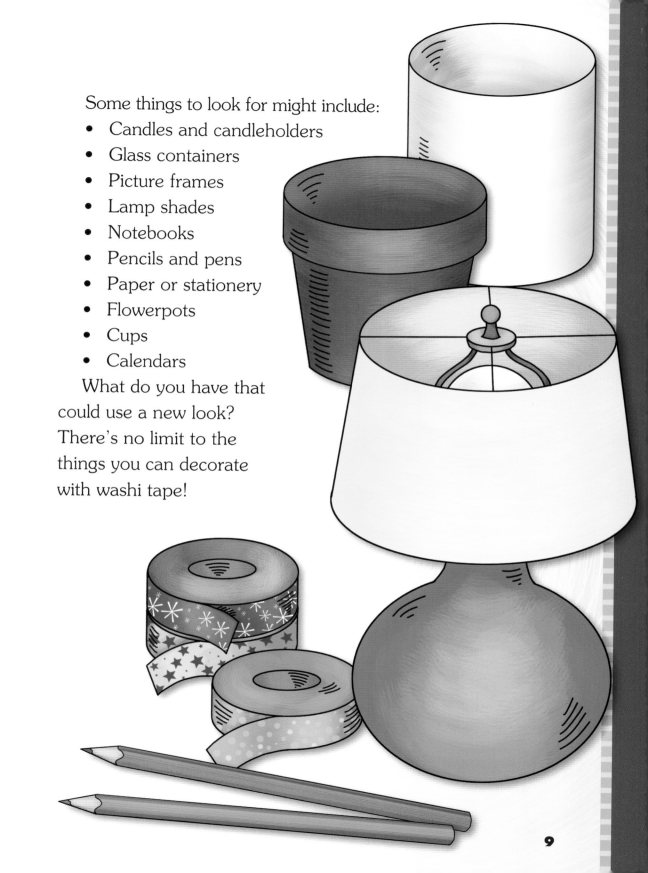

Some things to look for might include:

- Candles and candleholders
- Glass containers
- Picture frames
- Lamp shades
- Notebooks
- Pencils and pens
- Paper or stationery
- Flowerpots
- Cups
- Calendars

What do you have that could use a new look? There's no limit to the things you can decorate with washi tape!

Make Your Own Washi Tape

If you do not have a craft store near you, you can make your own washi tape. Many of the crafts in this book can be made using homemade tape. However, homemade tape does not peel off surfaces easily, so be careful where you stick it!

Materials
- Tissue paper, napkins, or wrapping paper
- Cutting board
- Double-sided tape (preferably with backing on one side)
- Mat knife or craft knife
- Straight edge
- Empty toilet paper roll

Steps
1. Choose the paper that you want to turn into washi tape. Spread it out facedown on the cutting board.
2. Carefully stick the double-sided tape to the back side of your

The back side of the paper should face up.

paper. Leave the backing on the front side of the tape if possible. Not all double-sided tape has backing. If yours does not, do not make the tape until you are ready to use it.

3. Ask an adult to help you cut the tape using the mat knife or craft knife. Use the straight edge to make your cuts straight and even. Make sure your paper is over the cutting board as you cut, so you do not ruin the surface of a table.

4. If your double-sided tape has backing paper on it, simply roll the tape you created around the empty toilet paper roll. You can roll several colors around one roll and use them when you are ready. If your tape does not have backing paper on it, you must use it as soon as you make it.

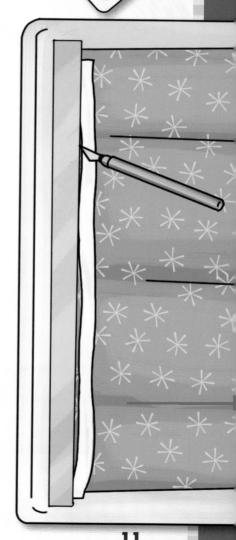

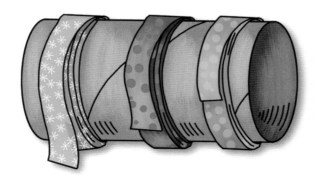

Pretty Pencils and Holder

Decorate your pencils in colorful patterns, then make a cool-looking holder to go with them.

Materials

- Old newspapers or old box
- White spray paint
- Glass jar or cup
- Washi tape (various colors and patterns)
- Scissors
- Box of colored pencils
- Pencil sharpener

Steps

1. Ask an adult to help you find a place where you can spray paint safely. Spread out newspapers or set down an old box to protect your work area from the paint. Use the white spray paint to cover the glass jar or cup. Let it dry.
2. Once the jar is dry, it is time to add stripes of washi tape. Begin by wrapping an even stripe around the bottom of the jar. Cut the

tape to size. Move up the jar as you decorate. Leave areas of white paint showing in between the stripes of tape. When you are done, set the jar aside.

3. Cut two pieces of tape to the length of a colored pencil. Lay one of the pieces sticky side up on the table. Set the pencil on the tape so that it reaches from the bottom to the top. Stick the tape to the pencil. Do the same thing with the other piece of tape to finish covering the pencil.

4. Repeat step 3 with all of your colored pencils. Use different colors or patterns for each pencil.

5. Sharpen your pencils after they are decorated. This will cut the edge of the tape perfectly with the wood on the pencil.

6. Store the pencils in the jar when you aren't using them. They'll give your desk a fresh new look!

Magnetic Ideas

These magnets are great for the refrigerator or inside your locker. They also make fun gifts for your friends!

Materials

- Old magazines
- Wooden craft circles or squares (chipboard works well, too; cut it into small squares or other shapes)
- Pencil
- Scissors
- Washi tape (various colors and patterns)
- Old newspapers
- Foam brush
- Glossy varnish
- Glue
- Magnets

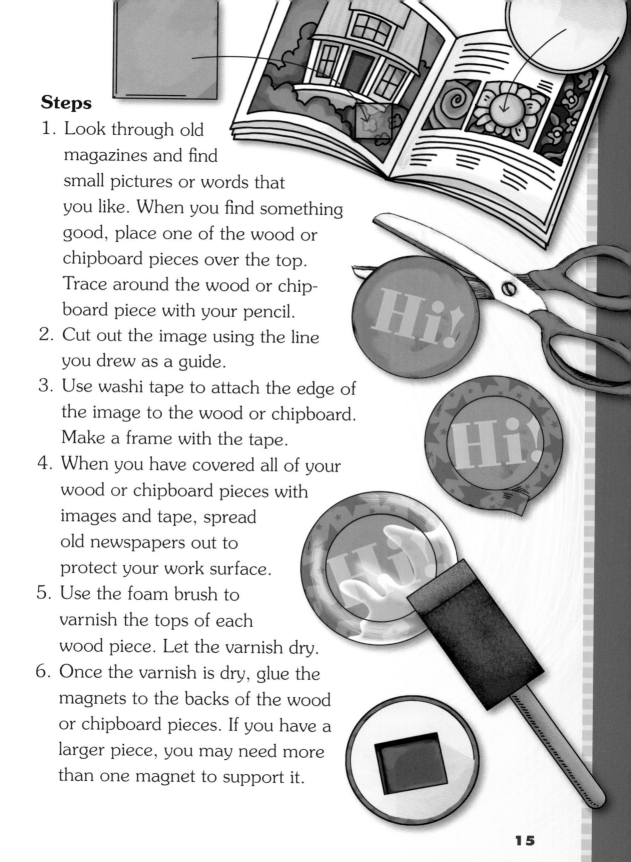

Steps

1. Look through old magazines and find small pictures or words that you like. When you find something good, place one of the wood or chipboard pieces over the top. Trace around the wood or chipboard piece with your pencil.

2. Cut out the image using the line you drew as a guide.

3. Use washi tape to attach the edge of the image to the wood or chipboard. Make a frame with the tape.

4. When you have covered all of your wood or chipboard pieces with images and tape, spread old newspapers out to protect your work surface.

5. Use the foam brush to varnish the tops of each wood piece. Let the varnish dry.

6. Once the varnish is dry, glue the magnets to the backs of the wood or chipboard pieces. If you have a larger piece, you may need more than one magnet to support it.

Abstract Wall Art

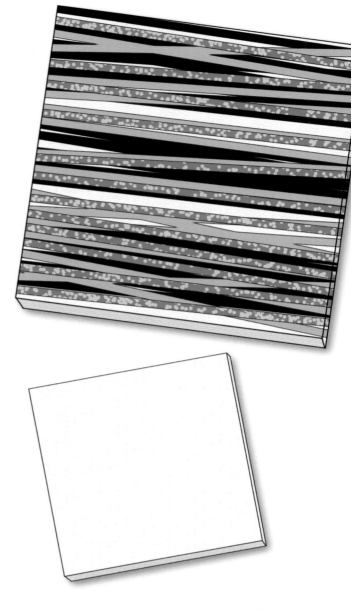

You can use washi tape to "paint" interesting designs onto a canvas. Create a whole gallery of unique artwork!

Materials
- Blank canvas
- Washi tape (various colors and patterns)
- Scissors
- Fine-tipped permanent black marker

Steps
1. Lay your canvas right side up on the table. Cut pieces of washi tape that are long enough to easily wrap around the edge of the canvas.

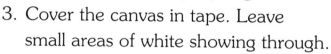

2. Stick the tape to the canvas at an angle. Continue to stick tape to the canvas at different angles across your canvas. All of the tape should go in basically the same direction (either horizontally or vertically), and all of the pieces should be slightly angled.

3. Cover the canvas in tape. Leave small areas of white showing through.

4. Stop adding tape once you are happy with the design. Flip the canvas over and trim all the edges of the tape to make them even with the back.

5. Turn the artwork over again so it is right side up. Sign the corner of the artwork using the fine-tipped marker.

6. Hang your artwork up for everyone to admire.

TIP
After you have made this project, you can try something completely different. Tape straight lines or make a checkerboard pattern next time. Cut your tape to make shapes. The possibilities are endless.

Bright Beach Accessories

Decorate your beach accessories with washi tape for a brand-new summer look.

Materials

- Washi tape (various colors and patterns)
- Old sunglasses
- Scissors
- Plastic flip-flops
- Compass
- Ruler
- Poster board
- Glue gun

Steps

1. Begin by decorating your sunglasses with tape. Wrap the tape around the arms of the glasses. You can also decorate the frames around the lenses by carefully cutting the tape to fit. Be sure not to tape over the lenses!
2. Next, decorate the bands of your flip-flops. The tape holds better if you wrap pieces around the bands instead of sticking long pieces along them. You can also add tape to

the edge of the flip-flop's sole. Cut the tape to make it even with the edges of the sole.

3. Now make a flower for each flip-flop. Use a compass and a ruler to make a circle with a 2-inch (5-centimeter) **diameter** on your poster board. Cut out the circle.

4. Cut a spiral into your circle. Start along the circle's edge and cut toward the center. Stop when you get to the center.

5. Wrap the spiral in tape. You can use different colors or wrap the entire thing in a single color. Make sure the entire spiral is covered in tape.

6. Pinch the center of the spiral and begin rolling the paper until you have a cone-like shape that looks like a blooming flower. This first roll will shape the flower.

7. Ask an adult to help you glue the flower. Unroll the paper and put a thin bead of glue around the center edge of the spiral. Roll up the flower again and hold it in place until the glue dries. Glue from glue guns dries quickly, but it can be hot. Be careful not to burn your fingers as you roll up the flower with the hot glue.

8. Glue your flower to the flip-flop.

9. Make a second flower for the other flip-flop. Now you are ready for the beach!

TIP

You can use washi tape to "paint" your fingernails to match your shoes and glasses. Simply cut the tape to fit the shape of your nails.

Designer Lamp

Create a lamp that is sure to get your visitors' attention. Use colors and patterns of washi tape that match the other decorations in your room.

Materials

- Old newspapers or old box
- Old lamp with shade
- White spray paint (if your lamp and shade are not already white)
- Washi tape (various colors and patterns)

Steps

1. If your lamp and its shade are not white, ask an adult to help you find a place where you can spray paint them safely. Spread out newspapers or set down an old box to protect your work area from the paint. Remove the lamp shade from the base of the lamp. Ask an adult to help you paint the lamp and shade white. Let them dry.

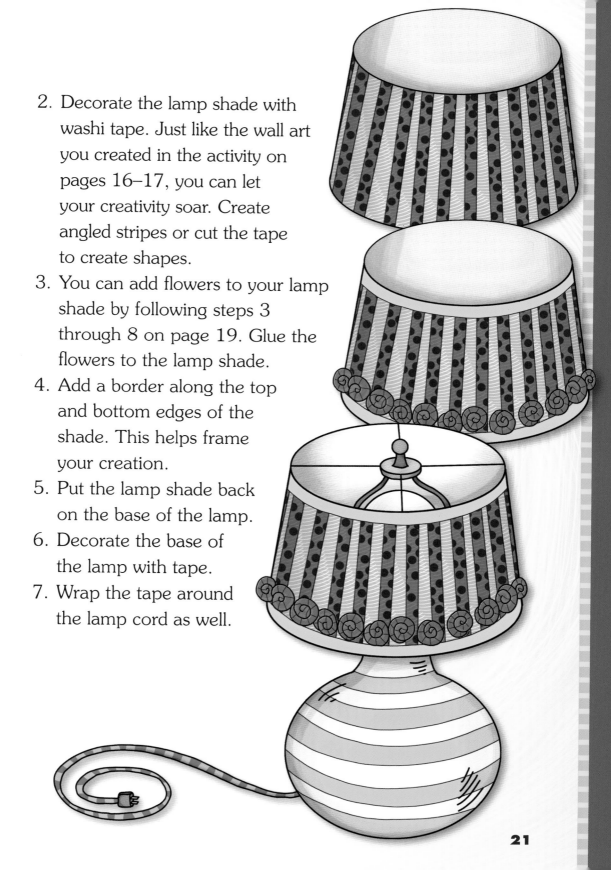

2. Decorate the lamp shade with washi tape. Just like the wall art you created in the activity on pages 16–17, you can let your creativity soar. Create angled stripes or cut the tape to create shapes.

3. You can add flowers to your lamp shade by following steps 3 through 8 on page 19. Glue the flowers to the lamp shade.

4. Add a border along the top and bottom edges of the shade. This helps frame your creation.

5. Put the lamp shade back on the base of the lamp.

6. Decorate the base of the lamp with tape.

7. Wrap the tape around the lamp cord as well.

Little Washi Tape Puppets

Create a cast of colorful washi characters and use them to put on puppet shows for your friends and family.

Materials

- Fine-tipped permanent black marker
- Wide popsicle sticks (one for each puppet)
- Colored markers
- Washi tape (various colors and patterns)
- Scissors
- Ruler
- Buttons
- Glue
- Compass
- Pencil
- Poster board

Steps

1. Use your black marker to draw a face, hair, and a neck on one end of a popsicle stick.
2. Color in the hair with your colored markers.
3. Choose a color of tape for your puppet's shirt. Wrap the tape on the popsicle stick from the base of the puppet's neck down about 2 inches (5 cm).
4. Glue buttons to the puppet's shirt. Use your markers to draw in a collar or pocket on the shirt.

5. Use washi tape to add a skirt or pants below the puppet's shirt. A skirt should be about 1 inch (2.5 cm) long. To make pants, add a stripe of tape to each side of the stick. Leave some bare wood in between the stripes.

6. For a puppet wearing a skirt, use your marker to draw legs and shoes. For a puppet in pants, draw shoes at the end of the pant legs.

7. Use a compass and a ruler to make a circle with a 2-inch (5 cm) diameter on your poster board. Cut out the circle. This will be your puppet's hat. Cover the circle in washi tape. Cut a slit in the center of the circle to match the width of the popsicle stick. You can make hats of all different shapes for your puppets. Be creative.

8. Stick the top of the popsicle stick into the slit and tape the hat in place from the back.

9. Make as many puppets as you like. Give all of your puppets names and personalities.

TIP
You can use a box to create a small puppet stage. Decorate the box with tape. Look through old magazines to find full-page photos of rooms in a house. Use the photos as backdrops for your puppet play.

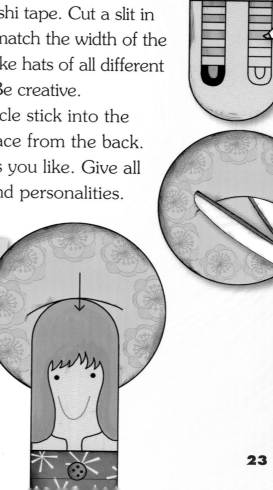

Washi Tape Checkers

Are you bored of basic, everyday checkerboards? Create your own custom checkers set using washi tape and other common craft supplies.

Materials

- Foam core (9.5 inches square, or 24 cm sq)
- 2 solid colors of washi tape (0.6 inches, or 1.5 cm, wide)
- 2 patterns of washi tape (0.6 inches, or 1.5 cm, wide)
- Scissors
- Mat knife or craft knife
- 24 bottle caps

Steps

1. Cover the foam core with 16 strips of one of the solid colors of washi tape. Start at one edge and make even stripes of tape all the way across the board. Wrap the tape around the board's edges. Do not leave space in between the tape stripes.

2. Choose a patterned washi tape and lay two stripes **perpendicular** to the ones covering your board. Place them along one edge of the board. Once again, wrap the tape around the board's edges and do not leave space between the stripes.

TIP

If your tape is 1.2 inches (3 cm) wide, cut your squares to a single (rather than double) tape width in steps 3 through 6.

3. Ask an adult to help you use the knife to cut through the top layer of tape and remove squares. Cut it using the bottom layer of tape as your guide. Two widths of tape make a square. Make the first cut two widths of tape down from the edge. Make the second cut two more widths of tape down. Remove the tape in the center.

4. Continue until you have eight squares. Four squares should be solid and four should be patterned.

5. Add two more rows of patterned tape next to the squares you just cut, carefully butting their edges together.

6. Once again, make cuts in the top layer of the tape every two rows, just as you previously did. This time, remove the opposite squares so you are left with a checkered pattern.

7. Cover the entire foam core in this checkered pattern. When you are done, you should have 64 squares—eight across and eight down.

8. Cover the tops of 12 bottle caps in the other solid-colored washi tape. Use your scissors to trim the tape to fit the tops of the caps.

9. Cover the remaining 12 bottle caps in the remaining patterned washi tape. Trim the tape with your scissors.

10. Place the solid-colored caps on the patterned squares. Place the patterned caps on the solid squares. Now you are ready for a game of checkers!

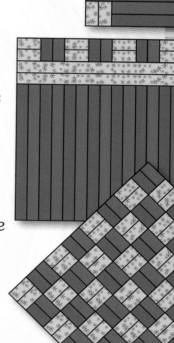

Creative Journaling

Create a colorful personal journal, a pen with a feather, and a ribbon bookmark. Use them to keep track of all your creative ideas.

Materials

- Blank journal or notebook (preferably with a light-colored, unpatterned cover)
- Washi tape (various colors and patterns)
- Scissors
- Old magazines
- Ribbon (8 inches, or 20 cm)
- Pen
- 1–3 feathers

Steps

1. If your journal has a flat spine, you can decorate the spine with washi tape. Start at the bottom of the spine and run the tape to the top. Cut the tape so it is even with both ends of the spine. If your journal has a spiral, skip this step.

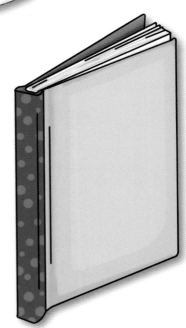

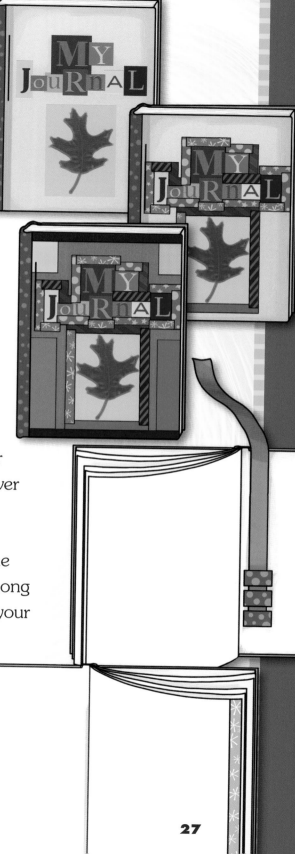

2. Page through your magazines and cut out small pictures and words that you like. Arrange the images and words on the front cover of your journal.

3. Use washi tape to secure the images along their edges, creating frames around each image.

4. Fill in the blank areas of your journal with more tape.

5. When the front of your journal is covered, flip it over and do the same to the back side.

6. After both sides are decorated, open up the back cover. Tape your ribbon to the inside of the back cover near the spine. The ribbon will be your journal's bookmark.

7. Turn the journal over and open the front cover. Run a piece of tape along the right edge of the first page in your journal. Cut the tape to match the length of the page. You can decorate as many pages in your journal with tape as you wish.

8. Set your journal aside and grab the pen. There are several ways to decorate your pen:

   a. If you have a clear pen where you can see the ink inside, take it apart. Cut a piece of tape to match the length of the plastic tube that holds the ink. Be careful not to break the tube and spill ink everywhere! Lay the tape sticky side up on the table. Place the plastic ink tube on top of the tape. Fold the tape over to surround the ink in colored tape. Cut the extra tape edge off. Put your pen back together.

   b. If your pen does not have a clear outer shell, decorate the outside instead. Make alternating stripes of colors and patterns to cover the pen.

9. Use the feathers to decorate the top of your pen. Cut a piece of tape that is about 2 inches (5 cm) long and place it sticky side up on the table. Stick the points of the feathers to the tape. Do not allow the bottom edges of the feathers to go below the bottom edge of the tape.

10. Stick the top edge of the pen on top of the feathers and even with the top edge of the tape. Wrap the tape around the top of the pen.

TIP

Sketch creative ways to use washi tape in your journal. Keeping a journal allows you to plan, revise, and make lists of materials for your projects.

Storing Your Tape

There are many creative ways to store your washi tape. Keeping all of your tape in one place makes it easy to find when you are ready to create something.

Materials

- Corrugated cardboard or foam core (3 inches square, 7.5 cm sq)
- Washi tape
- Rope (2 feet, 0.6 m)
- Pencil
- Wall hook or hanger

Steps

1. Use your pencil to poke a hole in the middle of the cardboard or foam core.
2. Decorate the cardboard or foam core square with washi tape. Put tape on the top, bottom, and sides of the board. Be careful not to tape over the hole.
3. String 3 inches (7.5 cm) of rope through the hole and tie a knot. Tie the knot large and tight so it will not fit back through the hole. Pull the string from the long end so the knot rests against the board.
4. String your rolls of tape onto the long end of the rope.
5. Hang the strung tape from a hook by wrapping the string around a hook on the wall. You can hang several ropes from one hanger or hook.

Have fun decorating things with all of your neatly sorted tape!

Glossary

adhesive (ad-HEE-siv) a substance, such as glue, that makes things stick together

diameter (dye-AM-uh-tur) a straight line through the center of a circle, connecting opposite sides

palette (PAL-it) a collection of colors

perpendicular (pur-puhn-DIK-yuh-lur) at right angles to another line or to a surface

pulp (PUHLP) the soft, wet mixture used to make paper

renewable (ri-NOO-uh-buhl) able to be regrown easily

For More Information

Books

Cerruti, Courtney. *Washi Tape: 101+ Ideas for Paper Crafts, Book Arts, Fashion, Decorating, Entertaining, and Party Fun!* Beverly, MA: Quarry Books, 2014.

Doh, Jenny. *Washi Wonderful: Creative Projects & Ideas for Paper Tape.* Asheville, NC: Lark Crafts, 2014.

Uhl, Robertta A. *Holiday Paper Crafts from Japan: 17 Projects to Brighten Your Holiday Season—Inspired by Traditional Japanese Washi Paper.* Rutland, VT: Tuttle Publishing, 2007.

Web Sites

Apartment Therapy—15 Washi Tape Project Ideas for Kids Rooms

www.apartmenttherapy.com/15-washi-tape-project-ideas-for-kids-rooms-184662

Visit this Web site for some inspiration on how to decorate your room with washi tape.

Washi Tape Crafts

http://washitapecrafts.com/

This blog is frequently updated with new ideas for washi tape creations.

Index

About the Author

Kathleen Petelinsek is a children's book illustrator, writer, and designer. As a child, she spent her summers drawing and painting. She still loves to do the same today, but now all her work is done on the computer. When she isn't working on her computer, she can be found outside swimming, biking, running, or playing in the snow of southern Minnesota.